Machines with Power!

Bulldozers

by Christina Leaf

BELLWETHER MEDIA
MINNEAPOLIS, MN

Blastoff! Beginners are developed by literacy experts and educators to meet the needs of early readers. These engaging informational texts support young children as they begin reading about their world. Through simple language and high frequency words paired with crisp, colorful photos, Blastoff! Beginners launch young readers into the universe of independent reading.

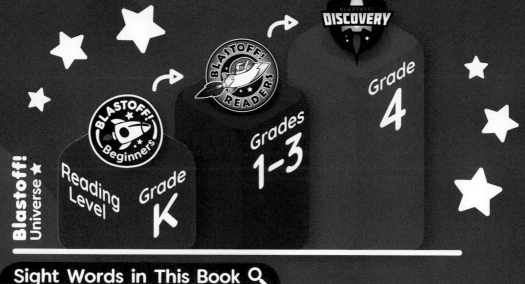

Blastoff! Universe ★

Reading Level — Grade K

Grades 1-3

Grade 4

Sight Words in This Book 🔍

a	go	of	this
are	help	out	up
at	here	sit	way
big	is	the	
come	it	these	
down	make	they	

This edition first published in 2021 by Bellwether Media, Inc.

No part of this publication may be reproduced in whole or in part without written permission of the publisher. For information regarding permission, write to Bellwether Media, Inc., Attention: Permissions Department, 6012 Blue Circle Drive, Minnetonka, MN 55343.

Library of Congress Cataloging-in-Publication Data

LC record for Bulldozers available at https://lccn.loc.gov/2020007060

Text copyright © 2021 by Bellwether Media, Inc. BLASTOFF! BEGINNERS and associated logos are trademarks and/or registered trademarks of Bellwether Media, Inc.

Editor: Amy McDonald   Designer: Andrea Schneider

Printed in the United States of America, North Mankato, MN.

Table of Contents

What Are Bulldozers?

Beep! Beep!
Out of the way!
Here comes
a bulldozer!

Bulldozers
push dirt.
They move rocks.

Bulldozers
clear paths.
They push
down trees.

Parts of a Bulldozer

This is the **blade**. It pushes big piles.

blade

U-blade

S-blade

These are
the **tracks**.
They go over
bumps.

tracks

This is the **ripper**.
It rips up
the ground.

ripper

This is the cab.
A driver sits here.

cab

Bulldozers at Work

This bulldozer helps make a road. It makes the ground flat.

This one works
at a **mine**.
It moves rocks.
Clear the way!

Bulldozer Facts

Bulldozer Parts

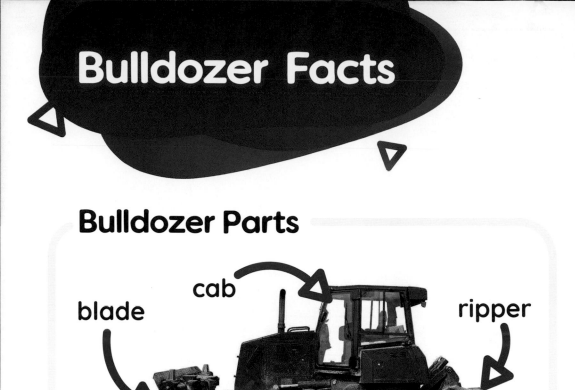

blade cab ripper

tracks

Bulldozer Jobs

move piles   clear paths   flatten ground

Glossary

23

blade

the part of a bulldozer that pushes and flattens

mine

a place where material is dug up from the earth

ripper

a sharp part that tears up the ground

tracks

parts that move bulldozers over ground

To Learn More

ON THE WEB

FACTSURFER

Factsurfer.com gives you
a safe, fun way to find
more information.

1. Go to www.factsurfer.com.

2. Enter "bulldozers" into the search box
   and click 🔍.

3. Select your book cover to see a list
   of related content.

Index

The images in this book are reproduced through the courtesy of: Odoirson Antonello, front cover; Pro-syanov/ Getty
Images, p. 3; MWP/ Alamy Stock Photo, pp. 4-5; TFoxFoto, pp. 6-7; Martin Haas, pp. 8-9; Juan-Enrique, p. 11
(U-blade); Stephen Mcsweeny/ Alamy, p. 11 (S-blade); swg3D, pp. 12-13, 22 (flatten ground), 23 (tracks); Taina
Sohlman/ Alamy Stock Photo, pp. 14-15; Jan van Broekhove, pp. 16-17; Joan Enrique del Barrio, pp. 18-19, 23
(blade); Thomas Moore/ Alamy Stock Photo, pp. 20-21; allo, p. 22 (parts); smereka, p. 22 (move piles); kviktor,
p. 22 (clear paths); Red Ivory, p. 23 (mine); AB Forces News Collection/ Alamy Stock Photo, p. 23 (ripper).